YOU CAN RESPECT DIFFERENCES

ASSUME
OR
FIND OUT?

You Choose the Ending

by Connie Colwell Miller • illustrated by Victoria Assanelli

Do you ever wish you could change a story or choose a different ending?

IN THESE BOOKS, YOU CAN!

Read along and when you see this:

WHAT HAPPENS NEXT?

Skip to the page for that choice, and see what happens.

In this story, Ben notices something different about Aisha. Will he ask her about her difference or will he assume? YOU make the choices!

Ben and his family are at a neighborhood cookout. Some kids his age are there. One girl is in a wheelchair. Ben has never met a kid in a wheelchair before.

WHAT HAPPENS NEXT?

→ If Ben does nothing, turn the page.
If Ben says hello to the girl, turn to page 20. ←

Ben wants to play basketball with all the kids. But he's not sure about the girl in the wheelchair. Should he ask her or not? He is afraid to talk to someone who looks different.

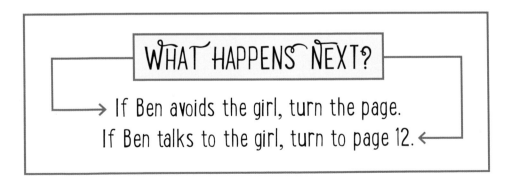

WHAT HAPPENS NEXT?

If Ben avoids the girl, turn the page.
If Ben talks to the girl, turn to page 12.

Before Ben talks to anyone, the girl wheels up to him. "Hi! My name's Aisha. What's yours?"

Ben says nothing. But Aisha isn't shy. She asks, "Do you want to play a game?"

WHAT HAPPENS NEXT?

→ If Ben refuses to play, turn the page.
If Ben agrees to play, turn to page 16. ←

Ben doesn't know what to do. "I don't want to play," he replies.

Ben walks off to find someone else to play with.

TURN THE PAGE

A few minutes later, Ben sees Aisha playing basketball
with a group of kids. Everyone looks like they are having
fun with Aisha. She can do cool spins with her wheelchair.

Now Ben wishes he had not assumed Aisha couldn't play.
He should have gotten to know her instead.

THE END

→ Go to page 23. ←

Ben is a little afraid, but he talks to Aisha. "I'm Ben," he says softly. "Why are you in a wheelchair?"

TURN THE PAGE →

"I have this chair," Aisha says, "because I have a
disease that affects my legs. The rest of me works
just fine though! I can show you."

Aisha shows Ben how she can play basketball in her
wheelchair. Ben thinks it's really cool! The two new friends
play basketball together.

THE END

↳ Go to page 23. ←

Ben does want to play. But he thinks Aisha might be too different. How will it work?

"What kind of games can you play in your wheelchair?" he asks.

TURN THE PAGE →

Aisha's face lights up. "I can play almost anything! Want to play basketball?"

Aisha shows Ben how she plays. At first, Ben is shy to play with her, but he warms up. The kids only have time for one game together. Ben wishes he hadn't made any assumptions.

THE END

→ Go to page 23. ←

Ben wonders about Aisha's wheelchair. But he tries not to assume anything about it. He talks to Aisha first.

"Hi, my name is Ben," he says to the girl. "Hi, Ben," she replies. "I'm Aisha. Do you want to play basketball?"

TURN THE PAGE →

Ben is surprised. "You can play basketball in a wheelchair?"
Aisha laughs, "Of course! Come on. I'll show you," she says.
Soon, the two kids are having fun together.

THE END

THINK AGAIN

- What happened at the end of the path you chose?

- Did you like that ending?

- Go back to page 3. Read the story again and pick different choices. How did the story change?

We are all different in some way, but some people's differences are easier to see. If you met someone different, would YOU make assumptions, or would you try to find out about the person?

AMICUS ILLUSTRATED and AMICUS INK
are published by Amicus
P.O. Box 1329, Mankato, MN 56002
www.amicuspublishing.us

Library of Congress Cataloging-in-Publication Data
Names: Miller, Connie Colwell, 1976- author. | Assanelli, Victoria, 1984-
author.
Title: You can respect differences : assume or find out? / by Connie Colwell
Miller; illustrated by Victoria Assanelli.
Description: Mankato, MN : Amicus Ink, [2020] | Series: Making good choices
Identifiers: LCCN 2018053329 (print) | LCCN 2018061131 (ebook) | ISBN
9781681517742 (eBook) | ISBN 9781681516929 (hardcover) | ISBN
9781681524788 (pbk.)
Subjects: LCSH: Discrimination--Juvenile literature. | Toleration--Juvenile
literature. | Respect--Juvenile literature. | Decision making in
children--Juvenile literature. | Judgment in children--Juvenile literature.
Classification: LCC HM821 (ebook) | LCC HM821 .M5555 2020 (print) | DDC
179.9--dc23
LC record available at https://lccn.loc.gov/2018053329

Editor: Rebecca Glaser
Series Designer: Kathleen Petelinsek
Book Designer: Veronica Scott

Printed in the United States of America
HC 10 9 8 7 6 5 4 3 2 1
PB 10 9 8 7 6 5 4 3 2 1

ABOUT THE AUTHOR

Connie Colwell Miller is a writer, editor, and instructor who lives in Mankato, Minnesota, with her four children. She has written over 100 books for young children. She likes to tell stories to her kids to teach them important life lessons.

ABOUT THE ILLUSTRATOR

Victoria Assanelli was born during the autumn of 1984 in Buenos Aires, Argentina. She spent most of her childhood playing with her grandparents, reading books, and drawing doodles. She began working as an illustrator in 2007, and has illustrated several textbooks and storybooks since.